Unlocking Your Strange Dreams
A Guide to Dreams and Dream Journaling

Copyright © 2024 by Lee J. Ashlin

All rights reserved. This book or any portion thereof may not be reproduced or used in any manner whatsoever without the express written permission of the publisher except for the use of brief quotations in a book review or scholarly journal.

First Printing: 2024

Because of the dynamic nature of the Internet, any web addresses or links contained in this book may have changed since publication and may no longer be valid.

Dedication

To the dreamers out there.

May your nights be filled with vivid adventures and your days enriched by the wisdom they bring.

Let your imaginations soar.

Contents

Preface 1
Thoughts On Why We Dream 5
Interpreting Dreams 11
Interpretation Symbols 15
Thatch 23
Daddy Longlegs 29
Healthy Sleep Habits 35
Topics of Discussion 37
The Benefits of Dream Journaling 41
Dream Journal Instructions 43
Dream Journal 45
My Strange Dream Journal 46
A Life of Strange Dreams 47
Advanced Dreaming 49
Dream Incubation 51
Lucid Dreaming 55
Group and Classroom Study 59
Group Dream Sharing 61
Lesson Plan for Teachers (Grades 5-8) 65
Lesson Plan for Teachers (Grades 9-12 and College) 71
Conclusion 75

Preface

When I was younger, my dreams intrigued me like reading a book or watching a movie. One particularly terrifying dream set me on the path to understanding them better. I was just a young child when I dreamt of a giant gorilla, towering over the trees behind my elementary school. The misty, damp forest, the eerie panicked bird sounds, and the screams of his victims left such a vivid impression that I can still picture it clearly, even over fifty years later. I was in awe of the feeling I had in that terrifying atmosphere.

In high school, my fascination with dreams only grew. I started making short films based on my dreams in filmmaking classes. It was a blast seeing these bizarre, otherworldly visions come to life on screen. Back then, I had to take a pin and physically scratch

My fascination with dreams only grew as I reached high school. I started making short films based on my dreams in filmmaking classes. It was fun to see these bizarre visions come to life. Back then, I had no special effects to make them look real. I had to take a pin and physically scratch multiple frames of film to make it look like a space ship from my dream was shooting lasers. I wanted to remember more of my dreams, but found most were elusive, slipping away from memory almost as soon as I woke up.

I soon learned how to recall my dreams and started keeping a dream journal. Some were scary, some violent, and others fun, but I could only remember the dreams that had just occurred as I woke up. With practice, I began waking up after each dream, sometimes experiencing four of them in a single night, to write down the details, including colors, sounds, and emotions. Over the years, documenting my dreams became a hobby, and I realized how interesting they were. I was able to retain them much better, and many even made good short stories.

But my curiosity didn't stop there. I wanted to understand why I was dreaming. Were these nightly adventures just random images, or did they hold deeper meanings? I couldn't shake the feeling that there was something more profound at play, something that could unlock the secrets of my subconscious mind. This determination led me on a journey of discovery, and now I'm excited to share what I've learned over the years with you.

This book will help you practice dream journaling and interpreting your dreams. You'll find a practical guide for understanding your own dreams, with insights into different techniques and methods for interpretation. Additionally, the book offers topics for group discussion, making it perfect for classroom settings or dream-sharing circles.

In this book, you'll find a practical guide to dream journaling and interpreting your dreams. I'll share insights into different techniques and methods for understanding your dreams, and you'll discover how to document them in detail. We'll dive into the history and significance of dreams across various cultures, offering fascinating insights into how societies have viewed and utilized dreams. You'll also explore the wonders of lucid dreaming, learning how to gain control over your dream narratives, and experiment with dream incubation techniques to intentionally influence your dreams.

Additionally, the book provides practical guidance on improving sleep habits to enhance dream recall and the quality of your sleep, which is crucial for vivid dreaming. Whether you're interested in personal reflection or group discussions, these tools will help you explore the hidden meanings of your dreams, uncover the layers of your subconscious, understand recurring patterns, and find deeper insights into the dreams that intrigue you.

As we journey deeper into the mysteries of our nightly visions, it's essential to explore the reasons behind why we dream. Understanding these reasons lays the foundation for interpreting and eventually influencing our dreams.

Let's journey into your dreams!

Thoughts On Why We Dream

The age-old question of why we dream has fascinated people for centuries, taking us on a captivating journey from ancient beliefs to modern science. Imagine one of our early ancestors jumping to his feet, thinking the woolly mammoth he just dreamed about is lurking nearby. Or the mystical sensation of a passed loved one appearing in their dream.

In today's world of advanced research, you might expect we have the answer to why we dream. However, the mystery endures, though we're making progress.

To understand how our ancestors thought about dreams, let's explore their varied beliefs shaped by their cultures and religions.

Take ancient Egypt, for example. They saw dreams as spiritual and predictive, a way for gods to communicate. As far back as 2000 BC, they wrote their dreams on papyrus and sought guidance from priests and dream interpreters to make important life decisions based on their dreams.

Similar ideas persisted in ancient Greece and medieval Europe. Both cultures believed that dreams could contain messages from the gods, but they also had more mundane explanations for dreams, such as the belief that they were caused by indigestion or stress.

Native American cultures had their unique take, viewing dreams as connections to the spirit world. Among the many tribes, the Ojibwe (also known as Chippewa) considered dreams to be powerful messages offering guidance and insights from the spirits. They believed that during sleep, the soul could communicate with supernatural beings, which was essential for spiritual health. One of their most significant contributions is the dreamcatcher, a handmade object with a web-like design, traditionally adorned with feathers and beads. Hung above the bed, dreamcatchers filter dreams, allowing good ones to pass through and gently reach the sleeper, while bad dreams are caught in the web and dissipated by the morning light.

This practice, rooted in an Ojibwe legend, has spread to other tribes and become a widely recognized symbol of Native American culture. Beyond the Ojibwe, tribes like the Lakota and Navajo also viewed dreams as essential means of receiving spiritual guidance and healing. The Lakota believed dreams were messages from the Great Spirit, while the Navajo saw them as communications with the Holy People. These practices highlight the central role dreams play in connecting individuals to the spiritual world and maintaining communal well-being across Native American cultures.

In ancient China, dreams were often seen as extensions of reality and a reflection of one's health and emotional state. Traditional Chinese medicine linked different types of dreams to the balance or imbalance of organs within the body. For example, the heart influenced dreams about joy or fire, while the kidneys were associated with dreams of swimming or water.

One of the most significant sources for understanding ancient Chinese perspectives on dreams is the Yijing, also known as the Book of Changes. This ancient divination text, which dates back over 2,500 years, contains 64 hexagrams that symbolize various states and processes of change. The Yijing was used not only for decision-making and predicting the future but also for interpreting dreams.

When interpreting dreams using the Yijing, the dreamer would identify elements of their dream and match them with the corresponding hexagrams. Each hexagram provided insight into the nature of the dream and its possible implications. For example, dreaming of water might be associated with the hexagram "Water over Water" (Hexagram 29), which signifies danger but also the possibility of finding a way through. By consulting the Yijing, individuals could explore the deeper meanings of their dreams and gain guidance on how to act in their waking life.

In addition to the Yijing, dream interpretation was influenced by various other cultural beliefs and practices. Dreams were seen as omens or messages from the spiritual world, and significant dreams could impact personal and political decisions. Overall, dreams in ancient China were an integral part of understanding the self and navigating the complexities of life.

In modern times, we're exploring dreams as problem-solving tools. They seem to help with memory and learning, especially during REM sleep. Dreams provide a safe space to process emotions and spark creativity and problem-solving. Interestingly, dreams often feature risky situations, perhaps preparing us to handle real-life threats through mental rehearsal.

From an evolutionary perspective, dreams may have helped our ancestors with social skills, problem-solving, and coping with dangers. This suggests our dreams today might continue this adaptive process.

Researchers believe that dreaming is essential for our well-being, just like sleep. They suggest that dreams can heal us by reducing the emotional impact of painful experiences. Dreams may provide a safe space to process upsetting memories and reach emotional resolutions when we wake up. Perhaps then dreaming is a form of overnight self-therapy, an evolutionary function that has helped us thrive.

So, what does all this mean? It means we still don't know why we dream, but we are on a possible path to understanding it better.

To me, I believe dreaming is my brain's way of coping with life in general. It sorts through my daily worries and ambitions, prepares me for future stress, and helps resolve my past worries, simulating real-life situations in sometimes very strange ways. Even if I don't remember them, I feel my daily adventures are broken apart and stored away deep in my brain to help me shape my personality to handle life.

I've always thought that waking up in the middle of a dream can feel a lot like the moment in "The Wizard of Oz" when Dorothy and her friends discover the man behind the curtain. In the movie, the Great and Powerful Oz declares, "Pay no attention to that man behind the curtain!" This scene is similar to our brain's intricate workings during dreams. In sleep, our brain weaves narratives and scenarios often shrouded in mystery and symbolism. But when we awaken abruptly, it's as if we catch a glimpse of the 'man behind the curtain'—the subconscious processes that usually remain hidden. This unexpected awakening can feel like a peek into the brain's backstage where the mechanisms of our dreams and subconscious are momentarily exposed, much like the unveiling of the ordinary man operating the grand illusion of Oz. Perhaps that's why our brain wants us to forget what we just witnessed so quickly.

Is there a metaphysical connection guiding our dreams? It's a fascinating question that invites us to ponder the unknown. Perhaps there's more to our dreams than meets the eye, a deeper unseen force at play. Anything is possible, I guess. I lean more towards a scientific explanation, but I will keep an open mind. As we continue to explore and understand our own consciousness, who knows what discoveries lie ahead? One day we may indeed find the answer, bridging the gap between the mysteries of our dreams and the unseen realms of the metaphysical world.

As you will read, I believe my dreams were preparing me throughout my life to overcome fear, forgive, love, embrace new situations, and alleviate my deepest worries. It also helped me to stay out of ice cream trucks with deranged, evil clowns. You can read that dream in my book "*A Life of Strange Dreams*" by Lee J. Ashlin.

Having explored various theories and cultural beliefs about why we dream, we can now study how these dreams can be interpreted.

Interpreting dreams can reveal much about our subconscious thoughts and emotions. What do you think your dreams are telling you? We will now review my approach to discovering the potential meanings of dreams.

Interpreting Dreams

When interpreting dreams, it's like peeling back the layers of a fascinating story. My dreams intrigued me. Each dream, whether scary, violent, or fun, held a unique narrative that faded quickly unless captured immediately when I woke.

The first step is to identify the very basics of the dream. Start with the main narrative and try to remove all the subplots. A monster is chasing you through the woods and you are terrified. You are walking through school and notice you are in your underwear and you are embarrassed. Why do you think you are dreaming this? Is it related to something going on in your life right now? Possibly. This should give you a base to build your interpretation.

Next, identify the key symbols in your dream. Think of these symbols as the central themes in a story. These elements are like the characters and settings in a novel, essential for understanding the plot. What do these symbols mean to you personally? A dog in your dream might represent loyalty, fear, or companionship, depending on your own experiences and feelings.

Emotions play a critical role in dream interpretation. Just as a good book evokes a range of feelings, your dream's emotions can offer profound insights. Reflect on how you felt during the dream and consider how these emotions relate to your waking life.

Patterns in dreams, much like recurring themes in a novel series, can signify unresolved issues or ongoing concerns. Look for these patterns to gain deeper understanding. Consider the context of your life at the time of the dream. Dreams often mirror your subconscious thoughts and feelings about real-life events and circumstances.

While dream dictionaries can be helpful and provide a general idea, it may not capture the full depth and nuance of your unique dream. Trust your personal interpretation, as dreams are highly individual.

Reflect on the possible meanings of your dream. Consider various interpretations, much like analyzing a complex storyline. What resonates with you the most? Dreams can have multiple layers of meaning, and the interpretation that feels right to you is usually the most significant.

For instance, when I dreamt that I was in the middle of a storm with multiple tornadoes, it reflected a situation in my life in which I had disruption and chaos between my mother and stepfather. The base of the dream was there were two tornados destroying everything around me. Those tornados were following me though time and I couldn't get away from them, very similar to the situation at home. When I was much older, I dreamt about UFOs, which can represent a desire to explore the unknown. The base of the dream was aliens arrived to take me to their home planet, but charging me too much for insurance. This made sense as I had an increasing desire to travel and see new things, but worried about the cost.

If you dream of flying, consider what flying means to you. It might represent a desire for freedom, an escape from responsibilities, or the feeling of achieving something great. Think about the context of your life. Perhaps you're feeling trapped in a job or relationship. Think about how this might influence your dream.

So, the basics of my approach are:
- Identify the very basics of the dream
- Try to connect dream content to things going on in your life.
- Look for dream symbols and their meaning.
- Put the pieces together on how the dream relates.
- Determine a possible meaning.

Interpreting dreams is a personal and subjective process, much like reading and analyzing a book. This is just my approach and nothing scientific. It seems to work for me. Trust your instincts, explore different meanings, and find the interpretation that resonates with you. Dreams are a rich source of self-reflection and insight, offering a window into your subconscious mind.

Sometimes, discussing your dream with others can provide new insights, much like discussing a book with a reading group. Friends, family, or even a professional therapist can offer different viewpoints that might help you understand your dream better. In later chapters we will explore group discussions.

Let's take this step by step and first learn some common dream symbolisms that typically appears in dreams. These will help build a base for interpretation of dreams. Then we will move on to some examples.

Interpretation Symbols

Start your dream interpretation journey with an open mind, knowing that each dream can have multiple meanings. Below are some common dream interpretations that can serve as a starting point. While there is still debate about the science of dream interpretations, these insights might reveal connections that resonate with you. Use these interpretations as a foundation and build upon them with your personal experiences and emotions. Can any of these interpretations help you see your own dreams from a different perspective?

Spiders: Can symbolize feelings of being trapped, anxious, or overwhelmed, especially if the dream involves fear or discomfort. This can reflect real-life worries or a sense of being ensnared in a particular situation.

House: A house often represents the self or the dreamer's mind. The different rooms can symbolize different aspects of the mind or different areas of the dreamer's life.

Water: Water typically signifies emotions and the unconscious mind. Calm water suggests peace and tranquility, while turbulent water indicates emotional turmoil.

Flying: Flying is commonly associated with freedom, control, and a higher perspective. It can reflect a desire to escape or a sense of liberation.

Chased: Being chased usually points to avoidance or fear. It suggests that the dreamer is running from something in their waking life, such as responsibilities or feelings.

Teeth: Teeth falling out often symbolizes anxiety about appearance or fear of embarrassment. It can also relate to a loss of power or control.

Falling: Falling is frequently connected to feelings of insecurity, loss of control, or fear of failure. It may indicate that the dreamer is feeling overwhelmed or unsupported.

Naked: Nakedness in a dream can reflect vulnerability, exposure, or feelings of shame. It may indicate a fear of being seen for who one truly is.

Vehicles: Vehicles like cars or buses symbolize a path in life or direction. Problems with vehicles can signify obstacles or a loss of control in life.

Animals: Animals in dreams can symbolize instincts, habits, or aspects of the dreamer's personality. Specific animals may have particular symbolic meanings (e.g., snakes for transformation or danger, dogs for loyalty).

Exams: Exams or tests typically indicate stress or anxiety about performance in waking life. They can also reflect feelings of being judged or evaluated.

Flying: Flying dreams can symbolize a sense of freedom and the ability to overcome obstacles. They may also reflect ambitions and a desire to rise above challenges.

Food: Food in dreams often signifies nourishment, whether physical, emotional, or spiritual. It can reflect the dreamer's desires, cravings, or what they feel is lacking in their life.

Money: Money in dreams usually relates to self-worth, value, or power. Finding money can signify discovering self-worth, while losing money can indicate feelings of inadequacy or loss.

Fire: Fire can represent passion, transformation, destruction, or purification. It might indicate strong emotions or significant changes happening in the dreamer's life.

Snakes: Snakes often symbolize fear, transformation, or subconscious worries. They can also represent healing or regeneration, depending on the context.

Bridges: Bridges in dreams often symbolize transitions, decisions, or connections between different aspects of the dreamer's life. Crossing a bridge can signify moving from one phase to another.

Mountains: Mountains typically represent obstacles, challenges, or goals. Climbing a mountain can symbolize striving for achievement or overcoming difficulties.

Keys: Keys are usually associated with access, control, or discovering secrets. Finding keys in a dream might indicate unlocking potential or finding solutions, while losing keys can suggest feeling locked out or restricted.

Tornado: A tornado in a dream symbolizes inner turmoil or a chaotic situation in your life. It reflects emotions and events that are approaching with intensity and potential upheaval, urging you to prepare for challenges.

Ocean: The ocean represents the vastness of your subconscious mind and emotions. It signifies deep feelings, unknown aspects of yourself, and the ebb and flow of life's experiences, urging you to explore your inner depths.

Alien: Seeing aliens in a dream indicates encountering unfamiliar elements within yourself or others. It reflects your willingness to explore the unknown, embrace diversity, or deal with situations that are beyond your usual understanding.

Guns: Dreaming of guns can suggest a range of emotions, from power and control to aggression and fear. The presence of a gun may reflect your need to assert yourself or your anxieties about confrontational situations.

Cats: Cats in dreams symbolize independence, mystery, and intuition. They represent feminine energy and your connection with your inner self. The behavior of the cat in the dream can provide insights into your emotions.

Police: Police in dreams embody authority, control, and rules. They can represent your conscience, feelings of guilt, or a desire for order and security. The presence of police may reflect your moral compass or fear of punishment.

Flood: A flood in a dream signifies overwhelming emotions or changes. It represents a flood of feelings that you might be struggling to manage. The dream urges you to confront and navigate your emotional landscape.

Forest: Dreaming of a forest symbolizes unexplored thoughts, desires, and growth. The dense trees can represent the complexities of your mind.

Storm: A storm in a dream represents turmoil and intense emotions. It reflects a situation in your life that is causing disruption and chaos. The dream invites you to acknowledge your emotions and find ways to navigate through the challenges.

Knife: Seeing a knife in a dream suggests the need to cut through problems or conflicts. It can also symbolize fear or a potential threat. The dream prompts you to address issues directly and make decisive choices.

Stranger: Encountering a stranger in a dream signifies new opportunities or unknown aspects of yourself. It can reflect your curiosity about the future or your apprehensions about unfamiliar situations.

Apocalypse: Dreaming of an apocalypse reflects fear of change, transformation, or the unknown. It might symbolize concerns about the future or a desire to escape overwhelming circumstances by starting anew.

Paralysis: Experiencing paralysis in a dream reflects feeling stuck or unable to move forward in a particular situation. It can symbolize emotional obstacles or a fear of being powerless.

Camping: Camping in a dream signifies a need for retreat and connection with nature. It reflects a desire to take a break from daily life, find solace, and rejuvenate your spirit.

Abandonment: Dreaming of abandonment indicates feelings of insecurity, fear of rejection, or unresolved issues from the past. It can reflect your emotional concerns about being left behind or not valued.

Abduction: Being abducted in a dream symbolizes powerlessness or fear of losing control. It might represent a situation in your waking life where you feel manipulated or trapped.

Acquaintance: Interacting with an acquaintance in a dream signifies exploring new relationships or connections. It can symbolize your openness to new experiences and expanding your social circle.

Baby: A baby in a dream represents new beginnings, potential, and vulnerability. It symbolizes nurturing and growth, urging you to embrace opportunities and take care of your aspirations.

UFO: Seeing a UFO in a dream indicates an interest in unconventional ideas or a desire to explore the unknown. It can symbolize your curiosity about things that are beyond your usual understanding.

Dog: Dogs in dreams represent loyalty, companionship, and friendship. They can reflect qualities you value in yourself or others. The behavior of the dog may offer insights into your relationships.

Ocean: The ocean symbolizes your deep emotions and the vastness of your subconscious mind. It reflects the need to explore your inner feelings and dive into your hidden desires.

Disease: Dreaming of disease reflects fears of illness or emotional distress. It might symbolize concerns about your well-being or the need to address issues affecting your mental or physical health.

Prison: Being in prison in a dream signifies feeling restricted or trapped by circumstances. It can symbolize your internal struggles or the need to break free from limitations in your life.

New Technology: Dreaming of new technology represents adaptation, progress, and innovation. It reflects your openness to change and your willingness to embrace advancements in various aspects of life.

War: War in a dream symbolizes internal or external conflict and struggle. It reflects challenges you're facing or your feelings about the competitive nature of your surroundings.

Virus: Seeing a virus in a dream reflects fears of contamination or vulnerability. It might symbolize your concerns about external influences affecting your well-being or stability.

Futuristic: Dreaming of a futuristic setting represents your anticipation of change and innovation. It reflects your outlook on the future and your interest in embracing new possibilities.

Childhood Home: Your childhood home in a dream symbolizes nostalgia, early experiences, and comfort. It reflects your connection to your past, family, and foundational aspects of your identity.

Rejection: Experiencing rejection in a dream signifies feelings of inadequacy or fear of not being accepted. It reflects your anxieties about being excluded or not meeting expectations in various areas of your life.

Haunted: Haunted houses can represent your own fears and anxieties. Dreaming about a haunted house can be a way to confront these fears and to learn how to manage them.

Death: Death can represent the end of something or a new beginning. Dreaming about a gunman killing someone may be a sign that you are going through a major change in your life.

Being Lost: You might be grappling with a situation where you lack a clear path or sense of purpose. This dream could reflect a fear of making the wrong choices, a sense of being overwhelmed, or a need to find your way back to a sense of security and stability.

Robots: Relates to the influence of technology in your life. This might reflect concerns about the increasing presence of technology or a fascination with technological advancements. It can also represent concerns about identity and authenticity. It can reflect feelings of being controlled or manipulated, or a fear of losing one's individuality and becoming more like a machine.

Doors: Doors in dreams often represent new opportunities, transitions, or access to new phases of life. Opening a door can symbolize entering a new stage, while a closed door might indicate an opportunity that is not yet available or a barrier in your path.

Mirrors: Mirrors in dreams typically reflect self-awareness, truth, and the way you perceive yourself. Looking into a mirror can symbolize self-reflection or a need to confront aspects of yourself.

Ladders: Symbolize progress, ascension, and reaching new heights. Climbing a ladder can indicate striving for success or personal growth, while descending a ladder might suggest exploring deeper aspects of the self or a retreat from challenges.

Phone Calls: Receiving or making phone calls in dreams can represent communication, connection, or a need to reach out to others. It can also indicate receiving important messages from your subconscious or addressing unresolved issues.

Shoes: Shoes in dreams can symbolize your approach to life and how you move forward. Wearing comfortable shoes might reflect confidence and ease, while worn-out or ill-fitting shoes could indicate struggles or discomfort in your journey.

Trees: Represent growth, strength, and life stages. A healthy, flourishing tree can symbolize personal growth and stability, while a withered tree might indicate feelings of stagnation or loss.

Books: Books in dreams often symbolize knowledge, wisdom, and the quest for understanding. They can represent learning, personal growth, or a desire to gain insight into a particular situation or aspect of life.

Elevators: Elevators in dreams can symbolize your progress in life, either moving up toward success and improvement or moving down into deeper aspects of your subconscious. Being stuck in an elevator may indicate feeling trapped or unable to progress.

Weddings: Often signify unions, commitments, and new beginnings. They can represent the merging of different aspects of yourself or significant changes and transitions in your waking life.

Roads: Roads in dreams usually represent your life path and direction. A smooth, straight road can indicate a clear and easy path ahead, while a winding or bumpy road might suggest challenges or uncertainties in your journey.

Windows: Can symbolize perspective, opportunities, and the ability to see things clearly. Looking out a window might indicate a desire for insight or a different viewpoint, while a closed window can represent missed opportunities or a limited outlook.

Animals: Can represent instincts, habits, or aspects of the dreamer's personality. Specific animals may have particular symbolic meanings (e.g., snakes for transformation or danger, dogs for loyalty).

Have you spotted any of these symbols in your dreams? There are countless more out there, each with its own unique meaning. A quick online search can uncover even more intriguing symbols.

Now, let's move to the next step using real dream examples and see how these symbols can help us interpret and understand the dream in the context of my life and the events unfolding at the time.

Let's take what we just learned and interpret a dream from my book, "*A Life of Strange Dreams*" by Lee J. Ashlin. It's just one example of a hundred dreams included in the book from three years old to my early sixties. It has a variety of dreams that are fun, like this one, to strange and unsettling. Most contain the date and time the dreams occurred as well as some information on what was going on in my life.

Thatch
11/29/16 6:10am

Dreams can often reveal underlying emotions and conflicts. For example, interactions with humanoid robots in dreams might symbolize feelings of loneliness or the desire for connection. Understanding these symbols can provide deeper insights into our subconscious mind.

To illustrate how these themes can manifest in dreams, let's explore a specific dream where a humanoid robot plays a central role. This dream reflects the complex emotions of loneliness and the search for connection, highlighting the interplay between the familiar and the unknown.

This dream was like a movie. I was observing it. It has some good emotions.

The weather was dreary in this fast paced, futuristic city, but people and robots travelled everywhere. There were still elements of an older city. Old brick buildings mixed with metallic modern skyscrapers and robots of various shapes and sizes walked the streets alongside people. The street was packed with all manner of vehicles. Transports floated over the roadways as flying drones zipped overhead. The air was thick with the sound of people and the hum of machinery.

The self-driven transports are crowded with both robots and humans. A brunette girl, in her early-20s, was sitting on a transport bench. The girl's gaze was fixed on the ground, her hair falling around her eyes like a curtain, shielding her from the world around her. Her vintage jeans and jacket were from a different era and didn't conform to the look of most residents, who were all dressed in sleek, futuristic styles. She looks sad and depressed, lost and alone; she seems unsure of her place in this world.

A robot steps onto the transport. He is humanoid in form, but does not appear quite human. His exterior comprises white metal, with some clear patterned elements across his body that revealed circuitry underneath. The circuitry glowed a warm blue color. His face could show a full range of emotions.

The robot stepped through the crowd to find a seat. As he sits down, he glances at the brunette girl sitting across from him. He observes her a few seconds before speaking.

"Hello", he says to her in a polite voice. She lifts her gaze just enough to see through her hair. She gives a half smile and looks back down at the floor.

He continues, "My name is Thatcher. Thatch for short. What's your name?"

Without looking up, she mumbles in an irate voice, "Christine".

"My owners are decent," he goes on, "they send me out on errands and I walk around this beautiful metropolis and discover fresh things and be around people. One of my job duties is feeding my owner's fish. I do this every night, including tonight!"

She seems uncomfortable and glances around for another seat. He detects this and says, "My apologies for talking too much. I just get excited when meeting unfamiliar people. I'm curious about you. What tasks do you do?

"Tasks?" She looks up and seems angry. "Well, let me tell you what tasks I do. I ride these transports looking for a place to fit in and don't feel a part of this city. I'm sad and worthless, do you understand? You're a robot and, no offense, don't have actual feelings, only programmed ones. Where are you going anyway?"

Her remarks surprised him. "I'm just finishing my errands and I exit this transport at the same place as you."

She asks with a bit of anger in her voice, "How do you know where I get off the transport?"

He pauses for a moment as he thinks. His glowing circuitry flickers a bit before he answers, "I am programmed to be honest, and so I will tell you the truth. I was riding this transport with my owner 1.2 months ago and I saw you in this very seat. I noticed you seemed lonely and in need of companionship and I am the same way. My owners are kind, but they own me. It's not the same as if I had an actual friend. I asked my owner if it would be all right to speak to you and he encouraged it, but you exited the transport before I could."

He continued, "Every day I ride this transport at the same time hoping to see you again and today I did. I hoped for us to be companions, but it seems I annoyed you and for that I am sorry."

She kept her gaze on him as he turned his face away. He seemed awkward and unsure of what to do or say. The transport stopped, and they both exited. She thought, "He seems sad, but how could that be?"

Exiting the transport, several other robots of all shapes greeted him with high fives as they passed by. He smiled at them, but seemed troubled. He looked back at her. Her gaze was down. His expression matched hers.

"I do wish to be a companion to you", he said as he lowered his head and turned away and began walking.

She raised her head and said, "So you're off to feed your owners fish?"

He turned back to her with a smile and replied, "Did I mention my owner's fish were artificial and don't really need to be fed?"

She shyly smiled as he walked up to her. She playfully bumped her shoulder against his and they walked away together, both smiling.

Interpretation

Step 1: Let's start with the very basics of the dream. A shy, introverted girl is struggling in a futuristic world and a robot is trying to be her friend. I'm thinking the girl character represents me because I have those traits, and the robot possibly represents technology or maybe another side of me reaching out to my introverted side. This gives me a good start, so let's move on from there.

Step 2: Connect dream content to things going on in my life. The dream unfolds in a fast-paced, futuristic city that blends the old with the new, reflecting a world in transition. It's like a mirror to my inner self, where the familiar past meets the unknown future. As I age, I'm trying to navigate the space in between, searching for my place. The presence of both robots and humans navigating this space together might represent my concerns about losing personal connections in a tech-driven world or the challenge of maintaining individuality.

Step 3: I look for dream symbols and their meaning. The vehicles in my dream, from ground transports to flying drones, symbolize life's journey, suggesting thoughts about the pace of life speeding up or feeling propelled by forces outside my control.

Step 4: I try to put the pieces together on how the dream relates to me. In this cityscape, Christine appears. Her vintage clothing embodies the feeling of being out of sync. She's adrift in a world that seems to have moved on without her. Her sadness speaks of a yearning for connection, a longing to belong. As I grow older, I feel this loss of connection and being out of sync with the current world. The pandemic, a few years after this dream, did not help my feelings of alienation.

Then there's Thatch, the robot, who exhibits human-like emotions. Despite his advanced programming, he grapples with loneliness. His honesty and desire for companionship bridge the gap between his artificial form and his genuine emotions. In him, I see a reflection of my own potential—the ability to connect, to find shared vulnerability, even with someone seemingly different.

Step 5: Finally, I determine a possible meaning. Their interaction, marked by a conversation about personal roles and tasks, goes deeper into these themes. Christine's struggle to find her place and Thatch's sincere attempts at friendship are conflicts between isolation and the need for friendship. This dream, to me, seems to be about purpose, acceptance, and overcoming the fear of progressing technology.

I believe this dream is telling me to embrace the very things that make us different to find new connections in my world. I need to be accepting of others in friendship while also keeping my techy side. It's about maintaining that balance between technology and real human connections, ensuring I don't lose either. I'm also sure at this time in my life I was being pushed into some new tech, and my subconscious was trying to help me deal with that worry.

Try not to think of what the dream is about on the surface, but what the symbolism and connecting threads are to your real life. As I age, I worry about keeping up with tech and not being useful. I don't want to be one of those seniors yearning for the past. I enjoy learning new things and try to keep a broad understanding of the world around me. I just don't want to lose the human connections as I age. Being more of an introvert, I can see this happening. I just need to keep pushing forward and stay connected.

This dream occurred before the current explosion of AI and the rapid changes it brings. In my current job, we are required to create uses for AI in our everyday tasks. I have no issues with this and enjoy it, but I still feel I'm always on the edge of tech getting ahead of me. I can see this scenario playing out in the near future with AI, with free-roaming robot bodies not far behind. Everything seems to be accelerating quickly.

If I push too much into tech, will I sacrifice true human interaction? With many of your dreams, you may find deep, underlying themes that resonate with your current experiences or emotions.

Let's do one more dream from

"A Life of Strange Dreams" by Lee J. Ashlin

Daddy Longlegs
7/1972

Interpreting dreams involves looking at various symbols and understanding their meanings. For example, spiders are a common symbol that can represent fears or anxieties. Each symbol in a dream can have multiple meanings depending on the context and the dreamer's personal experiences.

To better understand how these symbols manifest in dreams and influence our subconscious, let's examine a specific dream where a spider plays a central role. This dream, which I had during a summer visit to my grandfather's house in Tennessee, vividly illustrates how childhood fears can be exaggerated in our dreams.

I enjoyed visiting my grandfather in the summer. I had this dream while visiting.

As a Michigan native, I found it difficult to tolerate the sweltering heat of Tennessee during the summer. The humidity and heat made me feel like I was suffocating, but my grandfather seemed completely unaffected. His small white house, which had no air conditioning, was filled with a musty smell of old wood and mildew. Even the screened doors, which were supposed to let in a cool breeze, seemed to bring in more heat.

My grandfather was now a kind-hearted man that had not had a drink for many years. "Do you want to go fishing on the lake tomorrow?" he asked.

"Sure grandad!" The thought of fishing on the nearby lake always made me uneasy. The lake was once a valley that had been flooded after an earthquake, and as we rowed through the water, old underwater branches would scrape against the bottom of our boat, causing it to tip back and forth. I had not yet learned how to swim, and my sister had once told me that the flood had drowned a tribe of Native Americans. She claimed that those were not tree branches scraping against our boat but their skeletons reaching out to pull us down into their underwater camp. I tried to stay in the middle of the boat as much as possible.

"Why don't you go and get the fishing gear ready," he suggested. I walked to the back porch and stepped out the flimsy screen door, which slammed shut behind me. I found myself on a spacious screened porch with large windows that kept the Tennessee insects at bay. Crickets chirped in wire cages, waiting to be used as bait the next day.

I found the tackle box and began my search for the fishing poles. As I moved boxes around, I saw movement in the corner behind a stack of boxes. I took a nearby stick and prodded one box. As it tipped over, a giant Daddy Longlegs spider stood up. It's eight thin legs rose, revealing its bulbous body. It stood at least seven feet tall. I screamed in shock as its legs reached out.

My grandfather rushed through the door as I pointed to the monster. "It's just a spider", he said as a cigar in his mouth moved from one side to the other. "It won't hurt you." He picked up a broom and tapped it on its head.

"Go on now, shoo!" He tried to push the spider towards the door with the broom as its legs stumbled over boxes and other gear.

"Shoo. Go on. Get."

He slid a few things out of the way to make a clear path to the door. The spider moved around and reached for things in the cluttered area.

A few more taps on the head moved it through the path far enough where he could get behind it and push it along. The irritated spider hesitated, but finally cooperated.

He removed his cigar for a second to allow him to speak clearly, grinned, and said, "Open the door."

I moved in front of the spider and opened the screen door. I could hear the spring stretch and squeak as it opened. The spider scurried outside and letting go of the door; it swung shut with a satisfying bang.

Through the screen, I watched the spider walk away. I looked at my granddad. He was leaning over the broom, chewing on his cigar with a smile. With a slight laugh, he gestured in the direction of the spider, "Go on. Get."

Interpretation

Step 1: Let's start with the very basics of the dream. A giant spider, or threat, appears and terrifies me. My grandfather comes to the rescue in a very calm way and relieves my fears with his comforting presence. Now, let's go in further.

Step 2: Connect dream content to things going on in my life. The dream unfolds during a summer visit to my grandfather's house. Being already an anxious child, the fishing trip on a lake filled with my sister's eerie tales set the stage for nightmarish worries.

Step 3: I look for dream symbols and their meaning. According to dream interpretation symbols, I believe the giant Daddy Longlegs spider fits with me being overwhelmed by my fears, exaggerated to monstrous proportions. Its appearance on the cluttered porch, a place meant for safety, throws me into a state of panic.

However, the dream also highlights the comforting presence of my grandfather. His calm approach to the giant spider, brushing it away with a broom and his nonchalant commands, symbolizes reassurance and protection. Visiting my grandfather was always calming. His relaxed, friendly demeanor soothed my anxieties, providing great comfort amid the unpredictability and chaos of my home life, which would become even more dangerous in a few years. His ability to transform the terrifying presence of the spider into a manageable situation reflects the support and guidance he provided, even though I didn't get to see him often.

Step 4: I try to put the pieces together on how the dream relates to me. This dream captures my childhood experience of confronting overwhelming fears and finding comfort in the presence of a trusted adult. My grandfather's intervention, marked by his calm demeanor and practical actions, provides a sense of safety and reassurance, ultimately transforming the dream from a scene of terror to one of relief and protection. Guiding the spider out of the house and the door's satisfying bang as it shut behind it symbolized the transition from fear to safety.

Step 5: Finally, I determine a possible meaning. Reflecting on this dream, it becomes evident that my grandfather's influence helped me navigate my childhood fears, even if it was from a distance. The giant spider represents the various anxieties I faced, while my grandfather's composed handling of the situation signifies the guidance and support that helped me overcome these fears.

This dream shows how important it was to have a reassuring figure in my life and how childhood anxieties can be managed with support and protection, as it did for me. Just speaking to my grandfather over the phone would relax me, and I did that whenever possible.

Hopefully, after this dream, I felt more relaxed. I would continue my vacation adventures with my grandfather over the years with less anxiety and worry about my home life, knowing he would protect and help me if needed. Even if he was far away.

Dreams are a part of your inner world, waiting to be explored and understood. But before we dive into creating your dream journal, let's ensure you're properly set up and ready. Developing good sleep habits is crucial for vivid and memorable dreams. This means creating a restful environment, establishing a consistent sleep schedule, and adopting practices that promote deep, restorative sleep. When you sleep well, not only do your dreams become more vivid, but your ability to recall and interpret them improves dramatically.

So, let's take a moment to prepare your mind and body for the best sleep possible, setting the stage for a rich and insightful dream journey.

Healthy Sleep Habits

Good sleep habits are essential for improving both the quality of your sleep and the vividness of your dreams. By establishing healthy sleep habits, you can enhance your ability to recall dreams and ensure that your sleep is refreshing and fulfilling.

For instance, I always try to go to bed and wake up at the same time every day, which really helps my body clock stay on track. Creating a relaxing bedtime routine, like reading a good book or taking a warm bath, also signals to my body that it's time to wind down.

Creating a relaxing bedtime routine is super helpful. Activities like reading a good book, taking a warm bath, or doing some gentle yoga can signal to your body that it's time to chill out. Avoiding screens for at least an hour before bed is also important because the blue light from phones, tablets, and computers can mess with melatonin, the hormone that helps you sleep. Personally, I cheat a bit on this—I read with my iPad but use blue light blocking glasses. Usually, within 15 minutes, my iPad starts to fall out of my grip as I drift off.

The sleep environment plays a significant role in the quality of your rest. Make sure your bedroom is cool, quiet, and dark. Consider using blackout curtains to block outside light and earplugs or a white noise machine to minimize disruptive sounds. For myself, I use earbuds playing low volume, peaceful ambient music. A comfortable mattress and pillows tailored to your sleeping position can also make a big difference in how well you sleep.

Diet and exercise are important factors to consider as well. Regular physical activity can promote better sleep, but try to avoid vigorous exercise close to bedtime, as it can be stimulating. Additionally, be mindful of your diet; consuming large meals, caffeine, or alcohol in the hours leading up to bedtime can disrupt your sleep cycle. Instead, opt for light snacks if you're hungry and choose calming beverages like herbal tea.

Stress management is another key aspect of good sleep hygiene. Practices such as mindfulness meditation, deep breathing exercises, and journaling can help reduce stress and anxiety, which are common culprits of poor sleep. Engaging in these activities before bed can help clear your mind, making it easier to fall asleep and stay asleep.

Ensuring you get enough sleep is also crucial. Aim for 7-9 hours of sleep per night, as recommended by sleep experts. Adequate sleep allows you to experience multiple cycles of REM (Rapid Eye Movement) sleep, the stage during which vivid dreaming occurs. The more REM sleep you get, the more opportunities you have for vivid dreams.

Getting good sleep involves sticking to a regular schedule, having a relaxing bedtime routine, creating a comfy sleep environment, eating well, exercising, and managing stress. These habits not only help you sleep better but also make your dreams clearer and easier to remember. I've found that going to bed and waking up at the same time every day really helps me feel more rested.

With a solid foundation for quality sleep in place, it's time to explore the intriguing world of dreams and their meanings. Understanding the narratives, symbols, and emotions in our dreams can provide profound insights into our subconscious minds. In the next section, we'll explore thought-provoking questions to help unravel the complexities of your dreams and enhance your understanding of their deeper meanings.

Topics of Discussion

Dreams offer a mix of emotions, symbols, and narratives that can reveal deep insights into our subconscious minds. Analyzing dreams not only helps us understand ourselves better but also fosters engaging conversations and deeper connections with others. This section provides a comprehensive list of thought-provoking questions designed to guide your discussions and analyses of dreams, whether in a classroom setting, a dream-sharing group, or during personal reflection.

As you explore these questions, consider how each one can help unravel the complexities of a dream. Think about the emotions, settings, and symbols, and how they relate to your waking life. These topics aim to explore the dream, uncovering its possible meanings and the messages it might convey. Use these questions to spark meaningful dialogue, gain different perspectives, and enhance your understanding of the fascinating world of dreams.

What message do you feel this dream is trying to convey?

> This gets straight to the heart of the dream. What's the main takeaway or lesson here?

Think about the main feelings of the dream. How do you think the dreamer felt in real life at this time?

> Emotions in dreams often reflect real-life feelings. What was going on emotionally for the dreamer?

What would the dream tell you about the life of the dreamer at the time of the dream?

> Dreams often relate to our waking life. What clues does this dream give about what the dreamer was experiencing?

Was this dream a response to a threatening situation?

> Sometimes dreams are a way of dealing with fears. Was there something scary or stressful that this dream might be reacting to?

What interpretations can be applied to this dream?

> Let's brainstorm some possible meanings. What do you think this dream could be about?

Do you think the theme of this dream is common?

> Are these themes or situations something many people dream about, or is it more unique?

If the dream was interrupted, how do you think it could have continued?

> Use your imagination here. What might have happened next if the dream hadn't ended?

How did the dreamer interact with other people or things in this dream?

> Look at the dreamer's relationships and actions. How do they interact with the dream's elements?

Who was the antagonist in the dream?

> Every story has some conflict. Who or what was causing trouble in this dream?

Who was the protagonist in the dream?

> Identify the main character or hero of the dream. What role do they play?

What was the main conflict?

> What's the central issue or struggle in the dream? This is often key to understanding it.

Is it an internal conflict within the character?

> Is the dreamer struggling with their own thoughts or feelings?

Is it an external conflict caused by the surroundings or environment the main character finds themselves in?

> Or is the conflict coming from outside forces or situations?

What was the setting? Was it a geographic location, social environment, nature, or a combination?

> The setting can tell us a lot. Describe where the dream took place and think about its significance.

What symbols do you see in the dream that can be interpreted in another meaning?

> Dreams are full of symbols. What stands out and what might these symbols mean?

Do you see any patterns in the time or day of these dreams?

Are there specific times or patterns when these dreams occur? This can offer clues.

Focus on the actions taken by the dreamer or other characters. What do these actions symbolize, and how do they relate to real-life behaviors or desires?

Actions can be symbolic too. What might the dreamer's actions represent?

Discuss the lingering emotions upon waking. How do these feelings influence the dreamer's day or thoughts?

How does the dream leave the dreamer feeling, and how does it affect their day?

How could elements of the dream inspire creative projects or solutions to real-life problems?

Dreams can be a great source of inspiration. How could this dream spark creativity or solutions?

How does the dream reflect the dreamer's journey of personal growth or self-discovery?

Think about the dreamer's personal development. How does this dream reflect their growth or journey?

Many people write their lives down in journals, with the occasional, "I had a weird dream last night…" entry. Dream journaling is specifically for your dreams and encourages you to remember more of your dreams. Let's move on to how it can benefit you.

The Benefits of Dream Journaling

Dreams have captivated humanity for millennia, offering glimpses into our subconscious desires, anxieties, and hidden potential. But these fleeting visions often fade as soon as you wake. Dream journaling offers a powerful tool to capture these dreams, unlocking a treasure trove of insights that can benefit your life in surprising ways.

One of the most significant benefits of dream journaling is the boost it provides to self-awareness. By faithfully recording your dreams, you create a personal archive of your subconscious thoughts and feelings.

As you analyze recurring themes, symbols, and emotional patterns, you begin to understand yourself on a deeper level. Do you frequently dream of being chased? This might suggest unresolved anxieties or feelings of vulnerability in your waking life. Recognizing these patterns helps you address underlying concerns and cultivate greater emotional resilience.

Dream journaling can also serve as a potent source of creativity and often tap into realms beyond the constraints of logic and reason. Vivid imagery, fantastical scenarios, and unexpected juxtapositions can spark new ideas and fuel creative projects. Artists, writers, and musicians have long turned to dreams for inspiration. Authors like Stephen King and Mary Shelley have credited dreams with sparking the initial ideas for some of their most iconic works. My dreams have often inspired me to make short films, digital drawings, short stories, and more. By recording your dreams, you capture these sparks of inspiration before they vanish, allowing you to translate them into creative endeavors.

Furthermore, dream journaling can be a valuable tool for problem-solving. Stuck on a challenge at work or struggling with a personal dilemma? Dreams can offer surprising insights and solutions that might elude our conscious minds. By analyzing the symbolism and narrative of your dreams, you may discover new perspectives on a situation or even receive a nudge in the right direction. For example, dreaming of overcoming an obstacle could symbolize an upcoming challenge that you have the strength to conquer.

The benefits of dream journaling extend beyond these three key areas. It can improve your memory by strengthening your recall of not just dreams, but also daily experiences. Additionally, by processing your emotions through dream journaling, you can gain a sense of emotional release and improve your overall mental well-being.

So, the next time you wake up with a vivid dream lingering in your mind, don't let it slip away. Grab a pen and journal, and embark on a journey of self-discovery, creativity, and problem-solving with the guidance of your dreams.

Now let's explore how to make your own dream journals!

Dream Journal Instructions

Dream journals can assist you in remembering and interpreting your dreams. Copy or re-create the journal below, enlarging it if necessary. If you wish, you can keep it electronically, although I wouldn't recommend it as the bright glow of your electronic device could bring you out of your mind's dreamy state much quicker and you may forget parts of the dream or have trouble falling back asleep. It is better to have a pen and several sheets printed out and at the ready next to your bed and easily within reach. You don't want to move too much to retrieve them.

A useful technique is to tell yourself before sleeping, "I'll wake up after every dream." Persistence improves success. Once habitual, you'll likely wake after each dream to jot it down. A word of caution: When you wake up after a dream, don't say to yourself, "I'll remember it and write it down later in the morning." I've lost writing down many fantastic dreams this way. They just fade away.

Upon awakening, grab your pen and journal. Stay groggy and start immediately. Write the title. Maybe the first thing that pops in your mind. Don't spend much time on this.

Most people dream in full color, but quickly forget those colors, so sometimes you hear people say, "I just dream in black and white". Others report mostly pastel colors. Do you remember the colors in your dream? Circle the answer or note the vivid colors,

Glance at a clock, note date and time.

How are you feeling? Are you scared, upset, crying, happy, thrilled? Write them down. This helps me with the mood of the overall writing.

Now, describe your dream. The trick for me was to write as fast as possible and try to get all of the details. If I thought about it too much or tried to be a "writer", parts of the dream would begin to fade. The main goal is to get it all down on paper quickly. You can go back afterwards and fix your grammar, spelling, etc. Think of it as a very rough draft. Don't be afraid to use the back of the paper or another sheet. Keep writing until it's all out of your head.

Take your completed journal, move it to the bottom of the pile of blank journals, and place it nearby with your pen. If using an electronic device, save your work, get a new blank journal ready and place it nearby. You are now ready to the next dream. Go back to sleep and repeat throughout the night if possible.

The next day, go through your journals from the night before. Answer the last question on what's going on in your life at the time.

Now you can fix your errors and grammar and type it into your electronic device if you like. At this point you can be a writer, using your rough draft to make it flow properly. I find that during this phase I sometimes remember additional details about the dream.

At night before bedtime, start the process over again. Store them in a safe place and make backups of your electronic version!

One day, maybe 25 years later, you will go through them and be amazed on how your life was going and what dreams you were having at the time.

Dream Journal

Title: _____

Remember Colors? Yes/No_____

Date: _____   Time: _____   Emotions? _____

Describe Your Dream:

What is happening in your real life at this time?

My Strange Dream Journal

Part of the *Strange Dreams* Collection

Don't want to print out your own dream journals? I've crafted a journal for you!

Imagine a journal that's not just a notebook, but a portal to your dreams. Introducing *My Strange Dream Journal*, designed for the dreamer in you. With over 100 pages and space for **50 dreams**, it's your personal canvas to capture the landscapes of your subconscious.

It offers dedicated sections for expanding upon various dream elements, including emotions, life events, sketches, and more. The pages are adorned with charming moons and stars decorations that ignite creativity and provide direction for your journaling.

Keep it by your bed, and let your thoughts flow as you awake, preserving every detail before they slip away.

Visit
http://www.ALifeOfStrangeDreams.com
or scan QR code for more info.

A Life of Strange Dreams

Part of the *Strange Dreams* Collection

A fascinating journey into the dreaming mind.

From a young age, my dreams captivated me, unfolding like pages in a book or scenes in a film—some thrilling, some alarming, and others utterly delightful.

This book contains **100 dreams** spanning my lifetime, you can analyze the evolution of these dreams and how the themes shift with age. They read like short stories, although some can take odd turns. They are fun, scary, emotional, and strange.

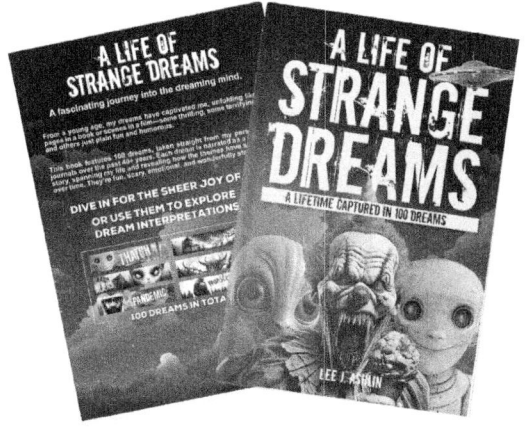

This is a great book to use **as a companion to this one** to learn and interpret my dreams as examples.

Or simply read them for fun!

Visit
http://www.ALifeOfStrangeDreams.com

or scan QR code for more info.

Advanced Dreaming

Now that you have learned about dream journals and interpretations, we can move into some advanced dreaming manipulation techniques. Dream Incubation helps you guide a dream before you fall asleep. Lucid Dreaming allows you to control the course of your dream while you are actively dreaming.

Both of these are advanced techniques and can take some time and patience to show results. When it does work, it can be very cool. I suggest you get very comfortable with dream journaling before you move on to dream manipulation.

Let's begin with Dream Incubation.

Dream Incubation

Dream manipulation, especially through dream incubation, is a cool way to influence what you dream about. The idea is to plant a seed in your mind about what you want to dream before you fall asleep. This isn't a new concept—ancient cultures used it to seek guidance, healing, or solve problems. Nowadays, people use dream incubation for personal insights and creative inspiration.

Dream incubation involves setting a specific intention before falling asleep. This can be achieved through various methods, including visualization, affirmations, and even writing down the desired dream scenario. The goal is to focus your mind on a particular subject or question, increasing the likelihood that your dreams will address it.

Have you ever wanted a sequel to a dream? This might help you achieve that. One time, I remember this working for me when I was dreaming that I was an inhabitant of an alternate, severely overpopulated world. Aliens landed and began eating everyone and multiplying. They allowed it to continue to thin out the population. I was eaten mid-dream, which startled me awake. I wrote the dream in my journal and wanted to continue it to see what happened next.

I used the methods in this chapter as I drifted back to sleep. I indeed found myself back at the point where I was eaten. But the dream took an unexpected turn: by being eaten, I was transported to an arena with younger versions of the aliens running toward me, and I was forced to dance ballet to keep them at bay. Yeah, let's move on to the technique. Haha.

One common technique is to think about a specific problem or question before bed. For example, you might repeatedly visualize a peaceful beach if you wish to have a calming dream, or think deeply about a work problem you need to solve. The process often involves a short meditation or relaxation exercise to clear your mind and concentrate on the chosen topic. Repeating a phrase like "I will dream about [specific topic]" can help reinforce your intention.

Scientific studies have shown that these methods can be effective. A study conducted by Harvard researcher Deirdre Barrett found that when participants focused on a problem before sleep, about half reported dreams that related to their chosen issue, and some even experienced solutions within their dreams (Barrett, 2001). This supports the idea that our subconscious mind can continue working on problems while we sleep.

Visualization is another powerful tool for dream incubation. Before you go to sleep, think about what you want to dream about. Visualize it clearly in your mind. This method taps into the brain's natural ability to simulate experiences and can be especially effective when combined with relaxation techniques.

Additionally, keeping a dream journal can aid in dream incubation. Jot down your desired dream scenario in your journal. This helps reinforce the intention in your subconscious. Also, by regularly recording your dreams, you become more attuned to their patterns and symbols, making it easier to direct them. Reviewing past dreams can also help identify recurring themes or symbols that you might want to revisit or alter.

While dream incubation can be an exciting way to explore your subconscious, it's important to approach it with a relaxed mindset. Stressing about whether the technique will work can be counterproductive. Instead, view it as a playful and exploratory activity.

When it works, it's fascinating. Even if you don't achieve your exact dream goal, you might still gain valuable insights from the process.

By setting a clear intention, using visualization and affirmations, and maintaining a dream journal, you can tap into your subconscious mind's problem-solving abilities and creativity. As research and personal experiences suggest, this practice can lead to fascinating and beneficial results, making your dream life a rich and insightful extension of your waking life.

Now, let's shift our focus to the exciting realm of lucid dreaming. You've learned tips on how to influence your dreams before you go to sleep. But what if you want to stay in your dreams and control them? This is where lucid dreaming comes into play.

Lucid Dreaming

In an upcoming chapter, you will learn tips on waking throughout the night to remember and write down your dreams in a journal. But what if you want to stay in your dreams and control them? This is Lucid Dreaming.

Lucid dreaming is like having a paintbrush to the canvas of your subconscious. As Carl Jung said, 'Who looks outside, dreams; who looks inside, awakes.' In this chapter, we will explore the fascinating world of lucid dreaming, where you can become the master of your own dreamscapes.

In all my years of dreaming, I've only had a handful of lucid dreams. Some occurred early in life when I learned to control and escape terrifying dreams by matching my body position in the dream with that in bed. One of my favorites was a dream where I fell off a cliff. As I hurtled towards the ground, I realized I was dreaming and began to fly. Soaring through the clouds like Superman, diving down city streets and back up again, it was a fantastic experience.

I must admit, I enjoy discovering where my dreams take me rather than controlling them. Therefore, I mostly adhere to the techniques for remembering and journaling dreams discussed in the next chapter. However, you might want to combine these techniques to occasionally realize you are dreaming and take control. Just have fun with it!

Lucid dreaming can be challenging, but practice and repetition can enhance your results. The science behind it indicates it occurs during the REM (Rapid Eye Movement) sleep stage, known for vivid dreams. It's crucial to recognize dream signs, recurring elements in your dreams that signal you're dreaming. Let's embark on a journey of lucid dreaming, where you become aware of your dreaming state. It can be an extraordinary experience, letting you explore the boundless realms of your imagination.

The first technique, **Mnemonic Induction of Lucid Dreams** (MILD), involves repeating a phrase like "I will remember I'm dreaming" as you fall asleep. This is akin to what you'll learn about remembering dreams in the next chapter. The difference is you'll be aiming to remember that you are dreaming, instead of the dream itself. You can also combine these, intending to remember the dream. This mental rehearsal can bolster your awareness in dreams, making it likelier to recognize the dream state.

One fun way to start having lucid dreams is by using something called **Reality Testing**. Basically, throughout your day, you get into the habit of asking yourself, "Am I dreaming right now?" and then do something to check. Try looking at a clock and then look away and back again—if the time changes drastically, you might be dreaming. Or, pinch your nose and try to breathe through it. If you can breathe, congratulations—you're in a dream!

Another technique, the **Wake-Back-to-Bed** (WBTB) method, which I wouldn't recommend on work/school nights due to the interruption of sleep, involves waking up after five hours of sleep, staying awake for about 30 minutes by reading or journaling, and then returning to sleep. This interruption in your sleep cycle can increase the likelihood of entering a lucid dream state.

The key is to notice when you are in a dream, the first step. While these techniques don't guarantee lucid dreaming, they lay a foundation for increasing your chances of experiencing this unique consciousness state. As you practice, you might notice dream signs, subtle cues indicating you're dreaming. These can range from out-of-place objects to unusual abilities like flying. Realizing you're in a dream allows you to start taking control.

Interestingly, research suggests activities like video gaming might help improve your ability to lucid dream, probably because of the focus and spatial awareness involved. Just like with remembering dreams, approach lucid dreaming with a balanced mindset. It's a skill that takes time to develop, so don't get discouraged if it doesn't happen right away. Also, remember that keeping good sleep habits is crucial for getting quality rest.

Lucid dreaming offers benefits like fostering creativity and problem-solving, overcoming nightmares, and enhancing self-awareness. It's can be used for confronting fears, exploring desires, and experiencing the mind's limitless possibilities.

As you continue to explore the fascinating world of dreams, consider the power of sharing these experiences with others. In the next section, we'll dive into the benefits and techniques of group and classroom dream study. Sharing dreams in a group setting can provide diverse perspectives and deeper insights, enriching your understanding of your own dreams.

Group and Classroom Study

Dreams have always been fascinating, not just personally but also when shared in groups. Discussing dreams in a group or classroom can bring new insights and interpretations that you might miss on your own. Group dream sharing lets you hear different perspectives, making the process more enriching and helping you see your dreams in new ways.

In a group setting, dreams become a shared experience, fostering a sense of community and connection. Participants can offer insights based on their unique experiences and backgrounds, which can lead to a deeper understanding of the dream's symbols and themes. This collaborative approach can reveal underlying patterns and messages that may not be immediately apparent to the dreamer. It also encourages empathy and support, as participants often find common ground in their dream experiences.

Classroom studies of dreams take this collaborative approach to another level, providing a structured environment for exploring the science and psychology behind dreaming. Students can learn about the historical and cultural significance of dreams, engage in discussions about dream theories, and practice interpreting dreams using various methodologies. This academic setting not only enhances their knowledge but also cultivates critical thinking and analytical skills.

Whether in a casual group or a formal classroom, the collective exploration of dreams can be both enlightening and transformative. It offers participants the opportunity to explore the subconscious mind, uncover hidden insights, and foster personal and collective growth. As you embark on this journey of shared dream exploration, you'll find that the experience is not only intellectually stimulating but also deeply enriching on a personal level.

Now that we've explored the depths of individual dream interpretation, let's take a look at how sharing these experiences in a group can bring new insights. Group dream sharing can reveal patterns and connections that might not be obvious when we dream alone enhancing our understanding through collective insights.

Group Dream Sharing

Group dream sharing is a collaborative activity where participants come together to share their dreams and engage in discussions about their possible meanings. In a group setting, each participant takes turns sharing a dream they've had, describing the dream's details, emotions, and any significant elements.

The group then engages in a collective exploration of the dream's symbolism and potential interpretations using one of the methods below. If they are uncomfortable sharing their dreams, one can be chosen from "*A Life of Strange Dreams*" by Lee J. Ashlin. Also, the leader of the group will need to determine if any dream subjects are off limits depending on the audience.

Dream Journal Sharing: Have participants share their recent dreams with the group. Encourage open discussion about possible interpretations, allowing different perspectives to emerge.

Symbol Exploration: Provide a list of common dream symbols. In pairs or small groups, participants discuss the potential meanings of these symbols in dreams, sharing their thoughts and insights.

Group Dream Mapping: Select a dream from one participant and create a visual representation of it on a large board or paper. Have the group collectively interpret the dream by discussing each element's significance.

Dream Role-Play: Assign participants roles representing different dream elements (e.g., dreamer, friend, teacher, stranger). Act out dream scenarios, encouraging participants to explore the interactions and emotions to gain insights.

Guided Imagery: Lead participants through a guided imagery exercise, prompting them to recall a recent dream. Encourage them to immerse themselves in the dream environment and emotions, aiding in interpretation.

Symbolic Art: Provide art supplies and ask participants to create visual representations of their dreams. Afterward, discuss the art and its potential interpretations within a group context.

Dream Sharing Circle: Sit in a circle and have each participant share a brief dream. The group collectively brainstorms possible meanings, offering insights and different viewpoints.

Dream Dialogues: In pairs, participants take turns being the dreamer and the interpreter. The dreamer presents a dream, and the interpreter asks questions to help the dreamer explore possible interpretations.

Dream Collage: Provide magazines, scissors, and glue. Ask participants to create collages representing their dreams using images and words. Afterward, share and discuss the collages as a group.

Group Symbol Dictionary: Collaboratively create a dictionary of dream symbols and their potential meanings. Invite participants to share their personal associations and experiences with each symbol.

Dream Debate: Choose a dream with ambiguous elements. Divide the group into teams advocating for different interpretations. Encourage a respectful debate that explores multiple viewpoints.

Dream Analysis Worksheet: Provide a worksheet with prompts for recording dream details, emotions, and personal associations. Have participants complete the worksheet and then share their findings with a partner.

Dream Interpretation Panel: Invite a panel of participants who have experience in dream interpretation to share their insights and methodologies. Open the discussion to questions from the group.

Additional Classroom/Group Exercises

The following are additional ideas and suggestions for a classroom or discussion group setting. You can either collect dreams from students or use the dreams in *"A Life of Strange Dreams"* by Lee J. Ashlin. Use these suggestions to advance the discussion of dreams as they relate to psychology, creativity, and how the human mind works.

Character Exploration: Give half the participants dreams featuring prominent characters and the other half dreams with less clear character roles. Discuss who the main characters are in each dream and what they might represent in the dreamer's life. Are they familiar faces or strangers?

Emotional Journey: Assign participants random dreams to read and trace the emotional progression throughout the dream. How do the dreamer's feelings change from beginning to end? Discuss how these emotional journeys might reflect the dreamer's waking life.

Recurring Themes: Read one dream to participants each day for open discussion. Focus on identifying any recurring themes or motifs in the dream. What might these recurring elements signify? Have participants determine if the themes are consistent with the dreamer's younger or older years.

Personal Symbols: Have participants document some of their dreams and then identify personal symbols unique to them that appear in these dreams. Discuss how these symbols differ from common dream interpretations and what they might mean to the individual dreamer.

Dream Logic: For homework, each participant chooses a dream that they feel relates to their life. In class, discuss how the dream's logic differs from waking reality. Are there any notable shifts in perspective or sudden changes that seem illogical? How might these dream logics provide insights into the dreamer's subconscious?

These exercises aim to deepen the fascinating world of dreams, encouraging participants to explore the rich tapestry of emotions, symbols, and narratives that can reveal deep insights into our subconscious minds. Through these activities, students and group members can foster engaging conversations, gain different perspectives, and enhance their understanding of dreams.

Now, before the final conclusion, I've included some lesson plans for teachers. This could also be adapted into adult group study sessions or your own personal learning experience.

Lesson Plan for Teachers (Grades 5-8)

Ever wonder what happens in your students' minds while they sleep? Dreams offer a fascinating window into their imagination, emotions, and subconscious. This lesson plan provides engaging activities to introduce students to the world of dreams, fostering curiosity about sleep, memory, and self-reflection. Through dream journaling, dream interpretation activities, and discussions about lucid dreaming, students will gain a deeper understanding of this mysterious aspect of human experience.

Lesson Title: Decoding the Night: Exploring the World of Dreams
Subject: Science/Health (can be adapted for Language Arts)

Grade Level: 5th-8th
Time Allotment: 90 minutes (can be split into multiple sessions)

Learning Objectives:

- Students will be able to define dreams and discuss their function.
- Students will understand the different stages of sleep and their relation to dreaming.
- Students will be introduced to the concept of dream journaling and its benefits.
- Students will explore various methods of dream interpretation.
- Students will learn about lucid dreaming and its potential benefits and challenges.

Materials:

- Whiteboard or projector
- Markers or pens

- Sticky notes (different colors)
- Dream journal template (optional)
- Images of different sleep stages (optional)
- Short video clip about lucid dreaming (optional)
- Copy of "A Life of Strange Dreams" by Lee J. Ashlin (optional)

Lesson Procedure:

Introduction (15 minutes):

Brainstorming: Begin with a brainstorming session. Ask students: "What are dreams?" Write their responses on the board. Discuss the different types of dreams (vivid, recurring, nightmares) and how they make students feel.

What is sleep? Briefly explain the different stages of sleep (REM and non-REM) and how they relate to dreaming. You can use visuals like pictures or diagrams to illustrate the stages.

Why do we dream? Pose the question: "Why do we dream?" There's no single answer, but discuss some possible functions like processing emotions, consolidating memories, or problem-solving. Use the chapter on "Why we Dream" in this book.

Activity 1: Dream Journaling (20 minutes):

Introduction: Explain the concept of dream journaling and its benefits, such as improving dream recall, self-reflection, and creativity.

Journaling Tips: Share some tips for effective dream journaling in this book. Encourage students to write down their dreams as soon as they wake up, even if it's just fragments. They can also include details like emotions, colors, and sounds. Use the chapter in this book "How to Dream Journal."

Design a Dream Journal (optional): If you have time, distribute a dream journal template or allow students to design their own journal pages. You can use the Dream Journal in this book.

Sharing (optional): For students comfortable with sharing, invite them to volunteer short snippets from their dream journals while keeping details anonymous.

Activity 2: Dream Interpretation (25 minutes):

Dream Symbols: Introduce the concept of dream symbols from this book and how they might represent deeper meanings. Explain that dream interpretation is subjective and varies across cultures. Use the chapter on "Why we Dream" and "Interpretations" in this book to help.

Symbol Activity: Divide students into small groups. Distribute sticky notes of different colors and brainstorm common dream symbols (e.g., falling, flying, water). Each group should write a symbol on a sticky note and stick it on the board. As a class, discuss possible interpretations for each symbol.

Personal Dream Analysis (optional): If time allows, students can write down a recent dream and analyze it using the brainstormed symbols and their own intuition.

Activity 3: Exploring Lucid Dreaming (30 minutes):

What is Lucid Dreaming? Introduce the concept of lucid dreaming, where the dreamer is aware they are dreaming and can sometimes control aspects of the dream.

Benefits and Challenges: Discuss potential benefits of lucid dreaming like creativity enhancement, problem-solving within dreams, and potentially reducing nightmares. Acknowledge potential challenges like difficulty achieving lucidity and the possibility of the dream becoming overwhelming.

Lucid Dreaming Techniques (optional): Briefly share some techniques for inducing lucid dreams, such as reality checks (pinching your nose) and the Mnemonic Induced Lucid Dream (WILD) technique (focusing on the intention to become lucid during sleep).

Video Clip (optional): If available, show a short video clip about lucid dreaming to provide students with a visual representation.

Wrap-up (5 minutes):

Briefly summarize the key concepts learned during the lesson.

Answer any remaining questions students might have about dreams.

Encourage students to continue their dream journaling and explore lucid dreaming techniques at their own pace.

Differentiation:

For advanced learners, provide research materials on different cultures' dream interpretations or explore the science behind dream research.

For struggling learners, offer sentence starters or prompts for dream journaling.

Modify the level of detail and complexity of the topics based on the grade level.

Assessment:

Observe student participation during discussions and activities.

Collect students' dream journals (optional) and provide feedback on their dream recall and journaling techniques.

Have students create a short presentation or writing assignment on a specific aspect of dreams that interested them most.

Extension Activities:

Students can create artwork inspired by their dreams.

Use dream journaling as a springboard for creative writing exercises. Students can write short stories or poems based on their dreams, focusing on specific elements like emotions, characters, or settings.

Research famous dreams that have impacted history or literature. Students can present their findings to the class and discuss the potential significance of these dreams.

Explore sleep hygiene practices that can improve dream recall. Students can create a "Dream-Friendly Nighttime Routine" infographic or poster to share with their classmates.

For students interested in lucid dreaming, have them research different techniques in more depth and experiment with keeping a "reality check" journal to track their progress.

Lesson Plan for Teachers (Grades 9-12 and College)

Teacher Introduction:

Are you looking for a way to spark critical thinking and discussion about the human mind? This lesson plan explores the science and psychology of dreams, offering a springboard for your high school or college students to explore this captivating topic. By examining historical and cultural perspectives on dreams, analyzing various dream interpretation methods, and discussing the phenomenon of lucid dreaming, this lesson plan will encourage students to critically evaluate the role of dreams in our lives and open doors for further research and exploration.

Lesson Title: Decoding the Night: A Deep Dive into Dreams (Higher Grades & College)

Subject: Psychology/Neuroscience/Literature (adaptable)

Grade Level: 9-12 & College Undergraduates

Time Allotment: 2-3 Class Periods (can be adjusted)

Learning Objectives:

- Students will explore the science of sleep and its connection to dreaming.
- Students will examine historical and cultural perspectives on dreams.
- Students will critically analyze various dream interpretation methods.
- Students will explore the potential of lucid dreaming and its applications.

Materials:

- Projector/Smartboard
- Markers/Pens
- Handouts/Articles on:
- Sleep stages and the neuroscience of dreaming
- Historical & Cultural Views on Dreams (optional)
- Dream Interpretation Theories (e.g., Freudian, Jungian)
- Lucid Dreaming Techniques (optional)
- Copy of "**A Life of Strange Dreams**" by Lee J. Ashlin (optional)

Lesson Procedure:
Introduction (30 minutes):

Review Basics: Briefly review the concepts of dreams, sleep stages, and their connection. Discuss the limitations of our current understanding of dreams.

Historical and Cultural Perspectives (optional): If time allows, explore how different cultures throughout history have viewed dreams. Include examples of dream interpretations and their significance within the specific culture.

Activity 1: The Science of Dreams (60 minutes):

Deep Dive into Sleep Stages: Use visuals and handouts to explore deeper into the different sleep stages (NREM 1-4, REM) with a specific focus on REM sleep and its association with dreaming. Explain the role of brain activity during these stages.

Neuroscience of Dreaming: Discuss the current scientific understanding of the neurological basis of dreaming. Explore theories on the function of dreams (e.g., memory consolidation, emotional processing).

Group Discussion: Divide students into small groups and assign readings on specific theories of dream function (e.g., Freudian, Jungian,

Information Processing). After reading, each group presents a summary of their assigned theory and leads a brief discussion about its strengths and weaknesses.

Activity 2: The Art of Dream Interpretation (45 minutes):

Is There a "Correct" Interpretation? Discuss the inherent subjectivity of dream interpretation and the lack of a universal "correct" way to understand dream meaning. You can use examples from the Interpretations section of this book.

Exploring Different Theories: Introduce various dream interpretation methods. Discuss the core principles of Freudian and Jungian dream analysis, highlighting the focus on symbols and archetypes. Explore alternative approaches (e.g., Gestalt Therapy, Associative Dream Interpretation).

Case Studies: Use dreams from the book "*A Life of Strange Dreams*" by Lee J. Ashlin for students to analyze. Present case studies for these dreams and ask students to apply different dream interpretation methods. This helps them understand how different methods can lead to diverse interpretations.

Activity 3: Exploring Lucid Dreaming (Optional) (45 minutes):

What is Lucid Dreaming? Introduce the concept of lucid dreaming and its potential benefits (e.g., creativity enhancement, overcoming nightmares). Discuss the challenges and ethical considerations associated with lucid dreaming.

Lucid Dreaming Techniques: Share different techniques for inducing lucid dreaming (e.g., reality checks, Mnemonic Induced Lucid Dream). Discuss resources available for practicing lucid dreaming techniques. See the Lucid Dreaming section of this book.

Debate (optional): Have students participate in a structured debate on the merits of lucid dreaming. Some points to consider could be the potential benefits versus safety concerns and the potential for manipulation of the dream world.

Wrap-up (15 minutes):

Briefly summarize the key takeaways from the lesson.
Open the floor for any final questions or discussions.
Encourage students to further explore specific aspects of dreams that piqued their interest.

Assessment:

Class participation during discussions and activities.
Short writing assignments analyzing personal dreams using different dream interpretation methods.

Research papers on historical or scientific aspects of dreams.
Creation of a presentation or infographic on a chosen topic related to dreams.

Differentiation:

For advanced students, provide materials on the philosophical implications of dreams or the role of dreams in literature. They can present their findings to the class.

For struggling learners, offer guided practice with dream interpretation methods using pre-defined dream examples.

Extension Activities:

Students can analyze the use of dreams in literature (e.g., Shakespeare's plays, surrealist poetry).

Research the ethics of using dream manipulation techniques in therapy or interrogation.

Explore the potential applications of lucid dreaming in fields like problem-solving or virtual reality experiences.

Conclusion

As we come to the end of this journey into the fascinating world of dreams, it's important to reflect on the insights and discoveries we've made along the way. Dreams are more than just fleeting images that pass through our minds while we sleep; they are profound expressions of our subconscious, offering us a window into our deepest thoughts, fears, and desires.

Keeping a dream journal has been incredibly insightful for me. It provides a wealth of information about my inner self and helps me understand who I am on a deeper level. By evaluating and listening closely to what my dreams are telling me, I can uncover my emotional state at different times in my life. This process allows me to recognize my strengths and weaknesses, and use these insights to tackle future challenges with greater confidence and clarity.

My dreams have been quite varied, ranging from evil mechanical sailor dolls, to sleepwalking and using a couch as a White Castle hamburger grill, to gut-wrenching dreams about my mother as she suffered through dementia. These dreams brought my deepest fears to the forefront, allowing me to confront and process them. They conditioned me to prepare for and overcome challenges, and then stored those feelings away as valuable lessons for the future. While everyone's experience with dreams may differ, many people find that their dreams serve a similar purpose, helping them navigate their inner worlds and face life's uncertainties with greater resilience.

By learning how to keep a dream journal, we've taken the first step towards understanding these nightly adventures. We've explored various techniques for interpreting dream symbols and themes, delving into the rich history of dream analysis across different cultures. From the wonders of lucid dreaming to the practice of dream incubation, influence their outcomes intentionally.

We've also seen how improving our sleep habits can enhance dream recall and the vividness of our dreams, creating a fertile ground for deeper exploration. And as we've ventured into group dream sharing and classroom studies, we've discovered the power of collective insight and the enriching experience of interpreting dreams within a community.

Dreams have the potential to guide us, heal us, and inspire us. They can provide clarity in times of confusion and offer comfort in moments of distress. As you continue to explore your own dreams, remember that each one is a unique reflection of your inner world, waiting to be understood.

As we conclude this journey into the world of dreams, remember that each dream is a unique reflection of your inner world, waiting to be understood. I hope this book has provided you with valuable tools and insights to continue your exploration of dreams. May your nights be filled with vivid, meaningful dreams, and may your days be enriched by the wisdom they bring.

Sweet dreams!

Lee J. Ashlin

Printed in Great Britain
by Amazon